Equity Investment for CFA level 1

CFA level 1, Volume 2

M. Imran Ahsan

Published by M. Imran Ahsan, 2020.

While every precaution has been taken in the preparation of this book, the publisher assumes no responsibility for errors or omissions, or for damages resulting from the use of the information contained herein.

EQUITY INVESTMENT FOR CFA LEVEL 1

First edition. May 21, 2020.

Copyright © 2020 M. Imran Ahsan.

ISBN: 979-8224892563

Written by M. Imran Ahsan.

Also by M. Imran Ahsan

ACCA
AACA: Business & Technology

CFA level 1
Corporate Finance for CFA level 1
Equity Investment for CFA level 1
CFA level 1 Fixed Income
Economics for CFA level 1 in just one week

Investment series
Corporate Finance: A Beginner's Guide
Fixed Income Securities: A Beginner's Guide to Understand, Invest and
Evaluate Fixed Income Securities

Dedicated to all knowledge and financial freedom seekers.

CFA level 1:

Equity investments

Complete Equity investments in 1 week

M. Imran Ahsan

Preface

Thank you for trusting us. This is another book for the CFA level one aspirants. We have used the same preciseness yet comprehensibility in preparing this book. It covers all the topics required for the Equity Investments CFA level 1. Usually the students complain that there is very lengthy study material for the CFA. This book intends to solve that problem, nevertheless this is most affordable with quality study material. This book is prepared very carefully to make the students feel happy about the whole course because they can easily grasp it now. So yes you should study and once again thanks for all the support and trust.

I am looking forward to come up with more books. Love you all the aspirants and may you succeed in your goals. Please don't hesitate to contact me about any issue.

M. Imran Ahsan

Ch.imranahsen@gmail.com

Whats app# 00923465006818

Study session 12 Equity investment (1)

READING 36. MARKET ORGANIZATION AND STRUCTURE

LOS 36a: Explain the main functions of the financial system.

Followings are major functions of a financial system;

Saving: Both individuals and companies set aside some amount of money to spend it later. Individuals may save during their working age to finance their retirements. Corporations may save for many different purposes like acquire other companies, install new plants, or to pay their lender or suppliers. This saved money can be invested into many types of investments from risk free T-bill to very risky corporate bonds. It is the financial system which transforms these savings into these investments.

Borrowing: The individuals and corporations who have not sufficient funds to finance their projects or needs can borrow from the depository institutes. These funds are to be paid back in future. People can borrow as secured or unsecured loans. The interest rate is high on unsecured loans. Individuals may borrow to finance for houses, cars and college education. Corporations may borrow to install new plant or to acquire other firms. Governments also borrow from domestic or international lenders. The lenders usually want collateral as a security to cover losses if the borrower defaults. The loans with collateral are called secured loans. There are some borrowings in which there is no collateral involved. These loans are called unsecured loans. The lender wants more interest rate as a premium as he is taking more risk.

Liquidity: This is the most important function of financial market. The liquidity means any asset is liquid if it can be bought or sold quickly without loss of value. The financial market provides this function. All other functions can be achieved in a good manner if the market is liquid.

Raising equity: For companies, instead of borrowing they can issue equity in exchange of future share in profits. The investment banks are involved to help the companies to issue the equity in market. The regulators regularize these offerings and perform a lot of other functions. In equities, the investor will not receive a fixed return but is promised to get return in form of dividends and capital gains.

Risk management: Derivatives like forwards, futures, swaps are used to manage the risks. Financial market provides these instruments to all types of investors.

Transfer of resources: The financial market provides the mechanism for quick and efficient transfer of almost all types of assets across countries.

Information: The financial market provides financial information to the investors. The investors who have information can earn excessive return. By using this information the investors try to buy at low and sell at higher prices.

Determine rate of return: The lenders want higher rate of return while the borrower want lower rate of return (cost of borrowing). The financial market equates the rate of return so that the demand for loan able funds is equal to supply of loan able funds. If the rate is too low there would be shortage of supply of funds and if the rate is too high there would be less demand for these funds. The financial market satisfies these two sides.

Efficient capital allocation: There is always scarce capital for the investment. The investors try to invest the funds in most preferred project (project with higher return). A well functioning, informed financial market allocates these resources in most efficient uses. In this way the market allocates the capital efficiently.

LOS 36b: Describe classifications of assets and markets.

Assets

Financial assets: These include equity securities, debt securities, derivatives and currencies.

- Equity: These are the stocks issued by different companies. These stocks can be public (being traded in stock market; public securities are subject to greater regulations) or private (stocks issued by private companies which are not being traded in stock exchange; private securities are subject to less regulations). Equity securities represent ownership in the entity who issued them.

- Debt securities: These securities are issued by different companies (even by governments) for a promised repayment of principal plus interest. Debt securities can also public as well as private. Debt securities do not represent ownership.

- Derivatives: These are the securities whose values depend on the value of other assets (discussed in derivatives in detail). Derivatives can also public as well as private.

Currencies: These are issued by central monetary authorities.
Commodities: These are physical goods like wheat, oil, gold etc.
Real assets: All tangible assets like property plant and equipments, timberland are real assets.

Markets

Primary and secondary market:
The market in which the companies issue their securities for the first time is called primary market. The subsequent issue or trade of securities between dealers and other market participants is held in secondary market.
Money market:
The market of debt securities with maturity of one year or less.
Capital market:
The market in which debt or equity securities with maturity of longer than one year are being traded.

Traditional investment market:

The market in which traditional investment instruments are trade.

Alternative investment market:

The market of hedge funds, real estate, rare assets etc is called alternative investment market. In this market the securities are less liquid.

LOS 36c: Describe the major types of securities, currencies, contracts, commodities, and real assets that trade in organized markets, including their distinguishing characteristics and major subtypes.

Assets can be classified into securities, currencies, contracts, commodities, and real assets.

Securities

Securities can be further classified into fixed income securities, equities and pooled investment securities.

Fixed income securities: These are debt securities which promise to repay the borrowed money with interest with a schedule. Many corporations and governments issue fixed income securities to raise funds. These securities can be short term (maturing in less than a year), intermediate term (maturing in two to five years) and long term (maturing in more than five years). {The cutoff date is used loosely}. Following are some major fixed income securities.

<u>Notes:</u> These are fixed income intermediate term securities.

<u>Bonds:</u> maturity of more than ten years.

<u>Convertible bond:</u> Hybrid security because it can be converted into equity.

<u>Bills/Securities of Deposit/Commercial Paper:</u> short-term securities.

<u>Repurchase Agreements:</u> Short term fixed income securities in which the borrower sells these instruments with a promise to repurchase at higher price.

Equity: These securities represent ownership in the corporation. Equity includes common stock, preferred stocks and warrants.

<u>Common stock:</u> Holder of common stock has the right of dividend issued by the company, right to elect board of directors and other payments in case of liquidity of company.

<u>Preferred stock:</u> Holder of preferred stock has the priority to get dividends but has no voting rights. The preferred stock holders get dividends before the common stock holders. Cumulative preferred stocks give the right to get any omitted dividends to preferred stock holders before the common stock holders get any dividend.

<u>Warrant:</u> Warrants gives the right to its holders to buy the equity (usually common stock) at a fixed price (called exercise price) before the warrants get expired.

Pooled investment: These are the investment vehicles which deal with different investments. These vehicles include mutual funds, exchange traded funds, hedge funds and asset backed securities.

<u>Mutual funds:</u> Mutual funds hold the securities of other companies. The investors can buy the securities of these funds directly from the funds (open end funds) or from a secondary market (closed end funds).

<u>Exchange traded funds:</u> These are like close ended funds. The investors can buy the shares of these funds in secondary market. Depository receipts are also indeed in this category.

<u>Asset backed securities:</u> These are the securities created (the process of creation is called securitization) from a pool of other securities. The pools of other securities can include car loans, mortgages, bonds and other credits. The income of asset backed securities is derived from pooled investment. These ABS have different priority claims.

<u>Hedge funds:</u> These are usually limited partnerships in which the mangers are general partners and the qualified investors are limited partners. These funds apply aggressive strategies to beat the market. These funds have two fee structures; management fee and incentive fee. Use of leverage is very common characteristic of these funds.

Currencies

Currencies are issued by central banks. The central banks also hold some reserve currencies in which the major international trades take place. The primary reserve currencies are US dollar, and Euro. The secondary reserve currencies include British Pound, Swiss Franc and Japanese Yen.

Contracts

These are the agreements to trade other assets in future. These assets can be currencies, commodities or other financial assets like shares. Contracts can be classified ad forwards, futures, swaps and options.

Forward contracts: Forward contracts are the agreement to trade an asset (called underlying) in future at a predetermined price and date. For example a contract to buy 100 kgs of Wheat in 90 days for $1/ kg is forward contract. Forward contracts are tailor made. They can be tailored according to the need of both parties. These contracts are over the counter contracts; they do not trade in secondary market (stock exchange or dealers market). That's why these contracts are considered illiquid.

Future contracts: These are like forward contracts but futures are not tailor made but standardized and they also trade in secondary market. So these are highly liquid.

Swaps: A swap is over the counter contract. In swaps two parties agree to exchange cash flows or liabilities. Generally one side cash flow is fixed and other side cash flow is variable .At the settlement date the net amount is paid to the concerned party. There is no payment at the time of inception of swap. The most common type of swap is interest rate swap and credit swaps to hedge (or to speculate) interest rate risk and credit default risks respectively. In credit swap one part gives periodic payments to another party and other party will pay the agreed amount to first party in case of credit default.

Options: The buyer (or owner) of call option has the right to buy underlying asset at predetermined price (strike or exercise price) for a specific time period (the position is called long call). The buyer or owner of put option has the right to sell the underlying at exercise price in a specific period of time (the position is called long put).

The seller of an option is called option writer. The seller of call option has the obligation to sell the underlying asset at exercise price in or on a specific time period the position is called short call). The seller of put option has the obligation to buy the underlying at exercise price in a specific period of time (short put).

At the inception of option the buyer pays option premium to the option writer. The buyer has no obligation except option premium. This option premium is called option price.

American option can be exercised at any time until expired. The European option can only be exercised at expiration. So the American option has different value than European (at expiration they are same for same underlying).

Commodities

Commodities include holding physical commodities like oil, metals and agricultural products. as well as owning the contracts related to these commodities like forwards, futures, options, swaps, commodity exchange traded funds, managed future funds, individual managed accounts, Specialized funds in specific commodity sectors and investments in the companies that deal with these commodities. Investment like these is made to get exposure in changing prices of commodities.

Real Assets

Real assets include lands, buildings and other residential, commercial properties, plants and machinery and also real estate backed debt like mortgage backed securities (MBS). These also include leveraged ownership of properties, real estate backed loans, and investment in Real estate investment trusts (REITs).

Income from real estate can include rental income as well as capital gains. Adding real assets in portfolio can reduce the overall risk and inflation hedge (the prices of real assets and rental income increases with rise in inflation).

LOS 36d: describe types of financial intermediaries and services that they provide.

Financial intermediaries

Financial intermediaries work between buyers and sellers of financial products. They facilitate exchange of capital and assets and risks. They increase efficiency in the market and ultimately help in economic growth. Following are major financial intermediaries.

Brokers: Brokers fill orders of their clients by finding the buyers or sellers and help to reduce transaction cost. Block brokers helps the large traders by placing their heavy orders. Large orders cause the market to move against the traders. The block brokers work in a way so their client lose lease amount of money.

Investment banks: These institutions help the corporations to raise capital by issuing many types of securities like shares and debentures. They also advise the companies about different matters like pricing the IPOs, acquisitions and mergers.

Exchanges: Exchange is a venue where the buyers and sellers meet and exchange financial assets. Exchanges also arrange trades coming from brokers and dealers. Exchanges also regularize their members (issuers, buyers and sellers) to promote efficient working of financial system. They require the companies to register with them and follow certain rules including periodic financial disclosures. The exchanges derive their authority from governments.

Alternative trading system (ATS)/ Electronic communication networks (ECNs)/ Multilateral trading facilities (MTFs): These work like an exchange except they do not have regulatory authority. Some ATS are also called dark pools as they do not show the orders of trade to other market participants.

Dealers: Unlike the brokers the dealers take the other side of trade with their clients. If a client wants to sell the dealers buy and if their client wants to buy the dealers sell. The dealers earn from the bid-ask spread. Dealers provide great deal of liquidity in the market. Some dealers also work as brokers called <u>broker-dealers</u>. There is a conflict of interest with broker-dealers. As a broker they need bed price for their client but as a dealer they need the price which increases their own profit. Clients put limit on orders while dealing with broker-dealers. Some dealers work with the government to buy and sell government securities as a part of monetary policy. These dealers are called <u>primary dealers</u>.

Securitization: Securitization is a process in which debt instrument like receivables, loans, mortgages etc. are purchased by an entity (called SPE or special purpose entity, special purpose vehicle or special purpose company) and then issues securities backed by those debts. The cash flows on newly issued security are backed by the cash flow from those debt assets (instruments). And the entities that do this are called securitizers.

Newly issued security in securitization can be of single class or multiple classes. In single class all securities are of same credit risk and holders of such securities have equal claims on assets. These different classes of asset backed securities (ABS) are called tranche. In tranche different classes of ABS holders have different claims on cash flows and the risk is redistributed.

Benefits

- The firm selling its financial debt can immediately raises capital to use.
- The backed illiquid financial assets (debts) are now liquid with new security. This new security can be traded in secondary market.
- The credit risk of the firm selling these assets is transferred to new entity.
- A financial company or bank is able to lend more with securitization. Without securitization the bank's lending was limited to traditional assets.
- The investors seeking to invest in debt have more options according to their risk tolerance and return.
- Securitization also increases the diversification which reduces risk.

Depository institutions: Commercial banks, saving banks, loan banks, credit unions and other related institutions are depository institutions. These institutions accept deposits from depositors (individuals and other entities) and lend it to the borrowers. They charge higher interest to borrowers and pay lower interest to depositors. The borrowing and lending spread is their income. These institutions also provide other services to depositors like checking accounts and transaction facilities. These institutions are experts in evaluation of credit quality and risk management.

Insurance companies: These financial intermediaries provide hedge against risk of a variety of losses (to individuals and corporations) and charge premium. These companies transfer the risk of buyers of insurance contracts to insurance company's shareholders and creditors. Insurance companies are also exposed to moral hazard (people act carelessly when they are insured), fraud and adverse selection (the problem that only most risky people buys insurance contract).

Arbitrageurs: When an asset is priced differently in different markets the market participants buy from low priced market and sell in high priced market and earns riskless return. This action is called arbitrage. Due to arbitrage the prices adjust quickly so the same asset would be priced same.

Clearinghouses: Clearinghouses arrange the final settlement of trade. They guaranty the final settlement of trade in future market and works as escrow (transfer cash and assets to respective party) in other market. To protect losses they require the members to have adequate funds to back their trades.

Custodians: They hold and protect the securities of clients from losses and fraud.

LOS 36e: Compare positions an investor can take in an asset.

Investor can have long position, short position or leveraged position.

Long position

An investor who owns an asset or has the right or obligation to purchase the asset in future under a contract is having long position. These investors can benefit from increase in price of assets. Under options a buyer of call option is in long position. Buyer of forward and future contracts is also holding long position. The investor with long position has the risk limited losses (up to the value of that asset) and the chances of profits are unlimited (the value of asset can increase up to any extent).

Short position

The investor who borrows the assets (usually stocks) and sell or an investor who has the right or obligation to sell under a contract in future is holding a short position. Short position holder benefits from a fall in price of asset. In this way she can buy at lower prices and cover her position. The seller of a call option or forward contract is holding short position. The selling of borrowed securities is called short selling. These investors have to clear their position within a specific time (repayment of the securities) is called covering the position. The borrower has to pay the dividends or interest income from borrowed securities to lender. These payments are called payments-in-lieu of dividends or interest. The short seller must also deposit the proceeds of sales to the broker as collateral. The broker also earns interest on these proceeds and a portion of this interest receipts may or may not be shared with short seller (at short rebate rate). The difference between short sale proceeds and short rebate is paid to the lender of securities. The short seller must also have to deposit additional margin to be eligible for short sale.

Leverage position

Buying of securities with borrowed funds is called leveraged position. The investors can borrow from broker and buy the securities. They can benefit from increase in asset's price. Buying on borrowed funds from broker is called buying on margin and loan is called margin loan. The borrower has to interest rate on these borrowed funds is called *call money rate*. Call money rate is usually higher than T.bills rate. The investors have to deposit a minimum amount at time of taking leverage position is called initial margin requirement. This initial margin requirement is decided by government, clearing house, exchange or any other regulatory body. This minimum margin requirement must be maintained. If any time the share's price falls below the initial / maintenance margin, trader will receive a margin call to deposit additional funds. If funds are not provided on margin call, the broker will close the position (sell the shares) to stop any further loss.

LOS 36f: Calculate and interpret the leverage ratio, the rate of return on a margin transaction, and the security price at which the investor would receive a margin call.

Leverage ratio: The leverage ratio of margin investment = Value of equity position ÷ Initial margin requirement

For example if a trader purchased the stocks of value $10000 and initial margin requirement is 50% (50 % of 10000 = 5000) the leverage ratio is 10000/5000 =2.

Rate of return on margin transaction: The rate of return is calculated on margin investment is same as calculating rate of return on any other investment adjusted for the interest payment or any other cost involved. It means we divide return by initial margin requirement or equity (not the value of purchased stocks) minus interest rate.

A complete example to calculate:

Share purchased 100

Per share price $10

Annual dividend per share $1

Initial margin requirement 50%

Call money rate 3%

Commission paid per share $0.03

Stock price after one year $12

Calculate the leverage ratio and rate of return on margin transaction.

Answer: The leverage ratio = 1/50% = 2

Total purchased value = 10 x 100 = $1000, initial margin or equity is 50% of this value so initial margin or equity (or investor's own money) is $500. The commission on purchase is 0.03 x 100 = $3. So the trader's total invested money is $503. Remaining $ 500 is borrowed money.

Total shares value at end of year = 12 x 100 =1200

Dividend received = 1x 100 =$100

Interest paid on borrowed funds = 500 x 3% = $15

Gain on shares = total value at end of year – value at time of purchase total initial investment - commission paid – interest paid+ dividend received = 1200 – 1000 - 3 - 15 + 100 = $282

The rate of return on margin transaction = 282/503 = 50.06%.

Margin call price: If the price of stock falls to this price level or below the trader would receive a margin call to deposit additional funds or un-margined securities to maintain margin level

$$\text{Margin call price} = \text{Initial purchase price} \times \left\{\frac{1-\text{initial margin requirement}}{1-maintinance\ margin}\right\}$$

or

$$\text{Margin call price} = \frac{\textbf{total borrowed funds}}{1-maintinance\ margin}$$

LOS 36 g: Compare execution, validity, and clearing instructions.
LOS 36h: Compare market orders with limit orders.

In dealer's market multiple dealers post the prices at which they are willing to buy and sell the securities. The price at which they are willing to buy is bid-price and the price at which they are willing to sell is ask-price. The size of bid and ask is also given along with the prices called bid-size and ask-size. Highest bid price and lowest ask price is quoted in the market. The difference between bid and ask prices is called bid-ask spread and the dealers earn from that difference. Same is true with shares and currencies. A trader has to accept the bid price to sell and ask price to buy. In brokered market the bid and ask can also be given by the counterparties (the traders). In most liquid markets the bid-ask spread is lower. The traders or dealers who post bid and ask prices are called market makers and the traders who trade with these quoted prices are called market takers.

While putting orders the traders can specify the size of trade, executions instructions, validity instructions, and clearing instructions.

Execution instructions

Execution means who t fill the order. Following instructions can be given with orders.

<u>Market order:</u> In market order the trader instruct the broker to sell or buy immediately a specific amount at the best available prices. This type of order fills immediately. It is suitable for those traders who want to execute their order at any price. Investors do this when they believe the market price is very low or very high or they have some information

which is not yet reflected in the market prices. The drawback of this type of order is the trader may get unfavorable prices.

Limit order: It is same as market order except the trader instruct about the minimum price to sell and maximum price to buy. If price goes beyond (above from that point for buy order or goes down from that specific price for sell order) the order will not execute (unexecuted or waiting to be executed orders are called standing limited orders). The drawback of this order is it might not be executed. A limited order between bid and ask prices is called making new market or inside market.

Marketable limit order: To make sure the execution of limit order an investor can put a buy order above the best ask price or a sale order below the best bid price. Orders of these types are called marketable orders or aggressively priced orders because at least some part of the orders must be executed.

Behind the market: A limited buy order below the best bid or a sale order above the best ask is called behind the market.

All or nothing order (AON): It is executed only if the whole order could be filled. It benefits the traders whose cost depends on the number of trades (not on number of share).

Hidden order: Orders which are not visible to other traders except exchanges and brokers. This order is good for the traders who put big volume to trade and they do not want others to see it. Because from large orders others can perceive the price change and the volume traders will get unfavorable price movements.

Iceberg order: The volume traders can also specify a display size from their order. In this order some of the volume is visible while remaining does not.

Validity instructions

Validity of an order means when the order will be filled.

Day order: These orders can only be executed in a day they are submitted. They will expire at the end of trading day in remained unexecuted.

Good-till-cancelled: As the name says these orders are open until executed or cancelled.

Immediate or cancel: These orders can only be filled immediately or cancelled.

Good-on-close order: These are only be filled at closing time of the market. These orders are usually submitted by mutual funds because their portfolios are valued by using closing prices.

Good-on-open order: Can only be filled at the opening of the market.

Stop sell order: These are sell orders and can only be filled if a security trades at or below the stop price level. It is used by investors to stop any further losses. Investors having long position use this type of order.

Stop buy order: These orders are only filled once the security is traded on or above the stop price. This type of order is submitted by a short seller who has to buy the security to cover her position.

The stop-sell and stop-buy orders are called stop orders or stop loss orders because they are used to stop further losses.

Clearing instructions

Clearing means how the trade is settled. Clearing instructions are not attached to each order but they are usually standing instructions. These instructions tell who will settle the trade. Retail trades are usually cleared by broker. Very big trades or trades of institutions are cleared by custodian or trader's prime broker. The clearing instructions also tell whether the sale order is short or long sale. In short sale the broker must confirm whether the securities can be borrowed or not. And in long sale the broker must confirm that the securities can be delivered.

LOS 36i: Define primary and secondary markets and explain how secondary markets support primary markets.

Primary market

In primary market to types of transactions held

1. The newly issued stocks of a firm whose shares are not being traded in other market. This is called initial public offerings (IPOs).
2. The seasoned offering: The issuing of new stocks by a firm whose shares are being traded in secondary market.

The issuer get help from an investment banker to find the buyer for seasoned as well as IPos.

The investment banks provide two types of offerings for sale of shares; underwritten offering and best effort offering.

With underwriting offering the bank agrees to buy any unsold shares at a pre-negotiated price. Under underwriting offering the investment bank has conflict of interest with the issuer. The issuer has hired the bank to sale its securities at higher prices but the bank want to reduce its own risk of buying unsold securities. Then bank wan to reduce the price and helps the buyers to buy the securities. under best effort offering the bank tries its best to sale the shares but if any number of sales are unsold the bank is not obliged to buy them.

The investment bank finds and attracts the investors to buy the securities by issuing the financials of the issuer. The investors who show indications of interest will be evaluated and sold the shares. The public issue of financials and getting indication of interest is called book building or book runner. If indication of interest is greater than the number of shares to be offered the price can be adjusted upward and vice versa.

Through **shelf registration** the issuer can sale the seasoned offering to the public over a period of time and when the market conditions are favorable.

Through **dividend reinvestment plan (DRP or DRIP)** the existing shareholders are offered to buy additional shares from their dividend at a discount. Through right offering the existing shareholders have the option to buy new shares at discount. These rights can be traded separately and can also be sold.

Through **Private placement** the new shares can be sold to qualified investors usually through investment banks. These qualified investors are those investors who have certain level of wealth and investment knowledge. Private placement cost is usually lower than public offering because the disclosures are less. The price of shares in private placement is also low because they cannot be traded in secondary market and offers lower liquidity.

Secondary market

In secondary market the trade happens without the involvement of issuer. In this market the buyers of IPOs and other offers, sale the securities to retail investors.

How secondary markets support primary markets

Imagine what would happen to primary market if there is no secondary market. The purchaser of original buyers cannot sale their ownership if they need money. The buyers would not available easily. The buyers from issuer will demand higher return (lower price) because of less liquidity. The issuer will get fewer funds. It is the secondary market which provides liquidity and the firms who are looking to raise capital can get best prices.

LOS 36j: Describe how securities, contracts, and currencies are traded in quote- driven, order-driven, and brokered markets.

Trading in securities market can be conducted through one of the following two ways. Call market and continuous market. In <u>call market</u> the trade is conduct at a specific time, at a specific price and all traders trade at same time. The traders declare the bid and ask rates and quantities which they want to trade. Then the price is negotiated and set in a way so all the securities can be traded at that price. The call market is very liquid in session because all potential traders are present in the market at that time. Between sessions call market is highly illiquid. The method of call market is usually used in small markets. This structure is also used by many governments to sell their securities like government bonds and notes etc.

In <u>continuous markets</u> the trades are conducted continuously when the market is open.

There are three categories of securities market; quote- driven, order-driven, and brokered markets. Buyers, sellers and dealers place their orders and their orders are matched according to some criteria. Most of the markets we see are continuous markets.

Quote- driven market / dealer markets/price-driven markets/ over-the-counter

Markets: In this type of market the investors or traders deal with dealers (the market makers). They quote bid and ask rates. Most of the trades in this market are conducted through electronic system or through phone. The dealers fill the orders from their own inventory or match the orders with other orders.

Order-driven markets: In this market the orders are matched using some rules. The orders are quoted by dealers and traders. Almost all the stock exchanges are order driven markets. The orders are usually placed anonymously. The buyers place the price at which they want to buy a specific quantity of securities whereas the sellers place the orders at which they want to sell a specific quantity. Following two rules are followed in this market.

<u>Order matching rule:</u> In the order-driven markets the highest bid and lowest ask are given the priority *(called order precedence hierarchy)*. If two orders of same price, the first arrived order is given the priority *(called secondary precedence rule)*. If a part of order remained un-executed the automatic system match it with next highest opposite order. These rules make the market continuous and promote liquidity.

<u>Trade pricing rule:</u> *Uniform pricing rule* is used in call market. Continuous markets use *discretionary pricing rule*. It means the price is discretionary. It determines the price base on the limit price of the first order or quote.

In *derivative pricing rule* the price is derived from another market (from main market or primary market) at a specific time in crossing networks. The price is independent of the orders submitted in crossing networks. Usually this derived price is average of bid and ask prices.

Brokered markets: Orders of unique assets are traded in this market. The market of these securities is illiquid and does not produce enough orders. In this market the brokers arrange trades. For example large block of shares and art work are traded in this type of market.

LOS 36k: Describe characteristics of a well-functioning financial system.

A well-functioning financial system with complete markets (markets having effective financial intermediaries and financial instruments) has following characteristics.

- Investors can save at fair rate of return
- Borrowers can obtain capital easily
- Hedgers can manage their risk
- Traders can exchange commodities currencies and any other asset easily

A well-functioning financial system has to be operationally and informationaly efficient. Operationally efficient means the financial system can solve the financial problems (borrow, hedging etc) at low trading cost. In informational efficient system the prices reflect all the available information due to timely disclosures. Due to well-functioning financial system the resources are allocated efficiently.

LOS 36l: Describe objectives of market regulation.

Without regulations the markets do not function efficiently. As a result the resources cannot be allocated efficiently and the economic growth is hampered.

The market regulations are required to prevent many problems like;

Fraud: The unsophisticated investors are easy prey for the investment firm and managers. The regulations are desirable to protect these investors from theft and fraud. Sometimes it is very difficult for the investors to calculate rate of return on their investment.

Insider trading: If there is insider trading, the investors will feel unsatisfied and they will not invest. As a result the market would be less liquid. The regulations prevent insider trading.

Agency problems: Regulations also solve agency problem by setting minimum standards for the brokers and investment firms (CFA and GIPS qualifications).

Default risk: Regulations also protect the customers from the misconduct of counter party (if counter party do not honor its part of the deal). Regulations require the market participants to have minimum capital before entering into a deal.

Financial reporting standards: Regulations require the firms to follow common financial reporting standards so an educated investor can obtain and analyze the information easily and cost effectively.

Prevent excessive risk: The regulations also prevent unqualified investors and firms to take excessive risk.

READING 37. SECURITY MARKET INDEXES

LOS 37a: Describe a security market index.

A security market index is used to gauge the performance of a market, an asset class or a segment of a market. An index is constructed by using a portfolio of securities. The securities included in an index are called constituent securities. Indexes can be constructed differently (we will discuss them later in this section) by using the actual or estimated (if not available) market prices at a point in time. Index return means percentage change in index for a particular period.

LOS 37b: Calculate and interpret the value, price return, and total return of an index.

Value of an index describes the changes in nominal values of index with respect to its base year.

Value of a price return index = VPRI = $\dfrac{\sum_{i=1}^{N} Nipi}{D}$

Where

VPRI = Value of price return index

N= number of constituent securities in an index

ni = number of units of a security in index

pi= unit price of i security

D= Value of divisor

Divisor can be any number usually in 000 to reduce the value of index to easily understandable.

When we calculate the price return we simple use deduct current index from previous index and divide it on previous index to get return in percentage form.

$$PRI = \frac{VPRI1 - VPRI0}{VPRI0}$$

Remember the price return only considers capital gain (price change).

In total return we consider both capital gain as well as other income from securities like dividends, interest etc.

$$Total\ return = \frac{VPRI1 - VPRI0 + other\ income}{VPRI0}$$

We can also calculate these returns by adding the weighted returns on each security in portfolio.

Rp= w1R1 + w2R2 + w3R3 ....WnRn

Rp= Return on index (price or total)

W1 = Weight of security 1 in portfolio

W2 = Weight of security 2 in portfolio

Wn= Weight of security n in portfolio

R1= return on security 1

R2= return on security 2

Rn= return on security n

LOS 37c: Describe the choices and issues in index construction and management.

Choices and issues in index construction and management: The index makers have to address following issues and make certain decisions while constructing and index;

- What is the target market the index is intended to measure? The target market can be broadly defined as "Asian stock market" or narrowly as "derivative market in USA". The market can be defined with respect to asset class, geographical location, exchanges etc.
- Security selection: Which securities should be included in an index and which should not be in the index.
- Weight: What weight can be given to each security included in the index.
- How and when the index would be rebalanced.

LOS 37d: Compare the different weighting methods used in index construction.

LOS 37e: Calculate and analyze the value and return of an index given its weighting method.

Following are some major weighting methods in index construction. Each method has its own pros and cons.

Price weighting: Price weighted index is constructed by including equal number of each security regardless of its price. Numerator is sum of all prices of securities in index and denominator is initially set as total number of securities.

Price weighted index = sum of all prices of securities/ number of securities

In this index the security with highest price has highest weight regardless of its market capitalization. So any increase or decrease in the high priced security will have more influence on index in comparison to a change in lowest priced security. When stock split happens, the divisor is adjusted in a way so the portfolio weight does not change. This index is very simple in calculation but the weights of securities are affected by stock splits, repurchase of stocks and by dividend issue.

Two famous price weighted indexes are indexes are the Dow Jones Industrial Average (DJIA) and the Nikkei Dow Jones Stock Average.

Equal Weighting: In equal weighting index same weight or importance is given to all securities included in the index. It is constructed in a way that same dollar amount is invested in all the securities. It means that there are fewer quantity of high priced security and more quantity of low priced security. This index is also very simple in calculation but requires more frequent rebalancing as the price changes. Financial Times Ordinary Share Index is weighted average index.

Market-capitalization weighted index or value- weighted index: This index is constructed according to market capitalization. The weight to a security is allocated according to following formula

Weight of a security = (number of outstanding shares x current market price) ÷ Total market capitalization

As *number of outstanding shares x current market price = market capitalization of that security.*

This index does not need changing or rebalancing due to stock splits and dividend issues, because weight of index stock is based on its market capitalization.

As the high cap companies are given more weight, this index represents the market better.

Drawback: As a company grows there would be a time where the market cap-index follower investors have to appoint huge amount of funds to a single company which will hinder the diversification. S&P 500 Index is capitalization-weighted index.

Float-adjusted market capitalization-weighted index: This index is constructed in same way except the weight is based on number of shares available to investors (excluding the controlling shares which are owned by directors and other parties who control the company).

For example weight of company A = number of shares of company A available to investors ÷ total number of shares of all companies available to investors.

Fundamental weighted index: In fundamental weighted index the weights are allocated according to the fundamentals of a firm like dividends, cash flows, revenues, book value and earnings. The weights in this index can be based on a single component like dividends or on a combination of different fundamentals. These weights are unaffected by market capitalization or share prices. So the market price biasness can be avoided. A company with higher cash flows will be weighted higher cash flows based index (Fundamental weighted index using cash flow weight).

LOS 37f: Describe rebalancing and reconstitution of an index.

Rebalancing:

Adjusting the weights of securities in an index on regular or interval bases (usually quarterly) is called rebalancing .Price and market- cap indexes usually do not need rebalancing as their weights are adjusted automatically. In case of stock splits the price- weighted index's divisor is needed to be adjusted. The rebalancing is the main concern for equal weighted index because with the price movements the weights changes.

Reconstitution:

Reconstitution is the process of adding and or deleting constituent securities in an index. The indexes are constructed according to a certain criteria (geography, sector etc.). If a security does not meet the index criteria nay more is replaced with another security which does. Mostly the reconstitution requires further rebalancing because adding a security drives up the price of that included security while deleting a security would drive down the price of that security. The main reason behind this is the followers of that index would also add and or delete those securities and the demand changes.

LOS 37g: Describe uses of security market indexes.

Market sentiments: The main and original function of an index was to gauge the market sentiment and investor's confidence.

Benchmark: An index can also be used as benchmark the performance of an active manager who follows the same securities as they are included in index.

Proxy for risk and return: Certain indexes set the expected return and risk profile for portfolio. The expected risk and return of individual security can also be calculated by using covariance and alpha.

Model portfolio: A passive manager or investor can invest in an index fund by using same weights. This way she can earn index return with lowest cost.

LOS 37h: Describe types of equity indexes

Broad market indexes: These market indexes represent more than 90% of securities in a market. Wilshire 5000 and Russel 3000 are broad market indexes. These indexes measure overall market performance.

Multi-market indexes: These indexes are constructed from indexes of different markets. They measure the market performance of a certain geographical location (i.e. Asian market) or using any other criteria like emerging market indices, or of entire world. For example For example, the S&P Global 1200 is multi-market index.

Sector indexes: These indexes are designed to measure performance of a certain sector in a country or in the world. For example energy sector index.

Style indexes: Indexes constructed on the basis of growth, market-cap and value or on a combination of these characteristics are called style indexes. For example small-cap growth index is a style index. The Russell 3000 Growth Index measures the performance of top 3,000 large-cap U.S.-traded stocks.

LOS 37i: Describe types of fixed-income indexes.

Companies, government and government agencies issue different types of fixed-income securities with different maturity, classes and preference of payment. So the universe of fixed-income securities and their indices is much wider than of shares. Fixed-income security indexes can be constructed on the basis of characteristics, geographical location, issuer etc.

Fixed-income securities are usually illiquid and sometimes index constructors need to contact dealers to obtain recent prices, which is a costly and time taking process.

LOS37j: Describe indexes representing alternative investments.

There are three main types of commodities indexes.

Commodity indexes: Commodity indexes include the future contracts of commodities. The underlying commodities can be precious metals, oil and other related goods. Different weighting methods are used in commodities indexes. These methods include equal weighting, fixed weighting and weight based on world production value. Some commodities may be included in different indexes but may show different risk and return profile due to the use of different weighting method. Another problem with commodity index is that the return on commodity index may be different from return of actual commodity itself, because the value of future contracts depends on roll yield and risk free rate.

Real estate indexes: These indexes include highly liquid real estate securities. Categories of real estate indexes are based on appraisal, repeat sales, or real estate investment trust (REIT) indices.

Hedge Fund Indices: Hedge funds are private investment vehicles which normally use leveraged funds, long-short strategies. Hedge fund indexes track the performance of hedge funds. Since hedge funds only report to private investors (and not to index providers), their inclusion in index is voluntary. The hedge fund indexes may be upward biased because only the highly performed funds will report to the index providers. Some funds may report to one index and not others so the performance of different indexes may vary. There is also an issue of survivorship bias because the funds who have managed to survive would be reported and the unsuccessful funds that are closed now will not be in an index.

LOS37k: Compare types of security market indexes.

Read LOS 37h to LOS 37 j as a whole for this LOS.

If you are enjoying this book so far kindly leave your honest reviews at
https://books2read.com/Equity-Investment-in-one-week-by-M-Imran-ahsan

READING 38: MARKET EFFICIENCY

LOS 38a: Describe market efficiency and related concepts, including their importance to investment practitioners.

Market is efficient if the prevailing prices reflect all the available information. The efficient market adjusts quickly to the information. The efficient market is very important to the active managers because they can exploit the information and earn extra risk-adjusted profits from passive investors, in inefficient market. In very efficient market the passive management is more desirable because "you can't beat the market" as the market already reflects the available information.

Efficient market is also important because it helps the resources to be allocated optimally.

Generally the markets are not hundred percent efficient neither totally inefficient. Different markets respond differently to new information.

LOS 38b: Distinguish between market value and intrinsic value.

Market value is the current market price at which an asset is being traded. The intrinsic value is the price a knowledgeable and rational investor is willing to pay for an asset.

If the market is efficient the market value is same as intrinsic value. However In inefficient market, as the prices does not reflect all available information the intrinsic value and market values differ. In this situation investors buy the assets which they value more than market price and sell the assets which they value less than the market prices.

One issue with intrinsic value is, it cannot be measured with certainty and it is continuously changing. Different investors use different methods to calculate intrinsic value.

LOS 38c: Explain factors that affect a market's efficiency.

Different markets respond differently to new information. Some markets absorb the information quickly and some markets respond slowly. No market is perfectly efficient or totally inefficient. Following are some factors that affect market's efficiency;

Market participants: More market participants increase the market efficiency and fewer participants contribute to less efficient market. Moreover highly sophisticated participants also increase the market efficiency.

Availability of information: A market, in which more information is available, tends to be more efficient. Usually markets of developed countries are more efficient than the emerging markets. As the information is plentiful, the insider trading can be highly discoursed which will increase the investor's trust and number of market participants increases.

Transaction and information costs: If the cost of getting information is low the market would be more efficient. Also when the transaction cost is low the market participants would trade reluctantly, which would contribute to more efficient market. Also with lower transaction cost the arbitrage opportunities could be easily and quickly exploited and the market prices will reflect all available information.

LOS 38d: Contrast weak-form, semi-strong-form, and strong-form market efficiency.

Professor Eugene Fama developed three forms of market efficiency; weak, semi-strong, and strong. Each form is based on the different set of information.

Weak-form market efficiency: This hypothesis states that the current market prices already reflect the historical data (prices and traded volumes). It means an investor using technical analysis (analysis based on historical prices and data) would not be able to earn abnormal profits. Weak form market efficiency is true in most developed markets but in less developed markets there are still opportunities to earn profits by using technical analysis because the markets are less efficient.

Semi-strong Form market efficiency: This hypothesis states that the current market prices reflect all the historical data and current new publically available information. Under this hypothesis, no investor can earn abnormal profit consistently by using publically available information because the market adjusts so quickly.

Strong-Form market efficiency: This hypothesis states that the current market prices reflect both public and private information including historical prices and volumes. An investor cannot earn consistently abnormal profits by using private information. This form is considered unrealistic, means no market is strongly efficient.

LOS 38e: Explain the implications of each form of market efficiency for fundamental analysis, technical analysis, and the choice between active and passive portfolio management.

Following table can exhibit whether the abnormal profits can be earned or not using different types of market efficiencies and management styles (active or passive)

	Technical analysis	Fundamental analysis	Active/passive management
Weak-form	NO	YES	Active
Semi-Strong form	NO	NO	Passive
Strong form	NO	NO	Passive

Weak-form market efficiency: This hypothesis states that the current market prices already reflect the historical data (prices and traded volumes). It means an investor using technical analysis (analysis based on historical prices and data) would not be able to earn abnormal profits. But investors using fundamental analysis and with active management style can still earn abnormal profits. This is because the market does not reflect the current information and active managers can exploit this opportunity.

Semi-strong Form market efficiency: This hypothesis states that the current market prices reflect all the historical data and current new publically available information. Under this hypothesis, no investor can earn abnormal profit consistently by using publically available information because the market adjusts so quickly. The active management style would only generate high costs as there are transaction costs and management fee is involved so the passive management is more desirable.

Strong-Form market efficiency: This hypothesis states that the current market prices reflect both public and private information including historical prices and volumes. An investor cannot earn consistently abnormal profits by using private information. In this market form the passive management is desirable.

LOS 38f: Describe market anomalies.
Market anomaly

It is a situation in which a security or a group of securities do not reflect all the current relevant available information. A market anomaly means some securities are not following efficient market hypothesis. This anomaly should be for longer period of time. A deviation from common rule for shorter period could exist in less efficient markets. Market anomalies can be grouped as time series, cross sectional, and others.

Anomalies in time series data

<u>Calendar anomalies:</u> Anomalies linked with different days, months or years are called calendar anomalies. The most common calendar anomaly is January effect. In January the stock tend to perform very well. This performance can be explained as the fund managers tend to sell

securities in December and buy them in January for the taxation issues or to show better financial results in December. Other calendar anomalies are weekend effect, turn-of-the month effect, and turn-of-the-year effect.

Momentum and overreaction anomalies: Momentum anomaly occurs when an asset's price rises (falls) it pushes the price to rise (fall) further. Overreaction anomaly is when a security has performed poorly in three to five years (3 to 5 is not a hard and fast rule), will perform better in coming years due to cognitive biasness (behavioral finance).

Cross-Sectional Anomalies

Size effect: It states that small companies have higher returns than larger companies or small-cap companies outperform the large-cap companies. In literature this effect existed until 1980s. It is argued that this was a random statistical result and does not actually exist.

Value effect: It is an anomaly that the companies which are being traded at lower P/E, Market to Book value ratios and higher dividend yield (value stocks) had outperformed the growth stock (with higher P/E, Market to Book value ratios and lower dividend yield). These stocks attract the value investors and they can drag the price up.

Other Anomalies

Closed-ended funds: Sometimes closed ended funds are being traded at a discount from their NAV. Future expectations about manager's performance, tax inefficiencies and transaction costs can explain these anomalies partially.

Earnings surprises: When stock price does not adjust to an unexpected announcement at-least at the same day. The traders can exploit this opportunity.

IPOs: IPOs are generally underpriced and the buyers of such stocks can earn excessive return. Sometimes the buyers drag the prices too higher than the actual price.

Most of the time these anomalies are result of statistical methods in use and overreaction/under-reaction of investors so trading based on these anomalies could not be always profitable.

LOS 38g: Describe behavioral finance and its potential relevance to understanding market anomalies.

Behavioral finance is the study which examines how investors and financial analysts make decisions and the effects of their decisions on the market. It concludes that the market participants are not always rational and they suffer from different biasness (in opposite to economics/ finance assumption of complete rationality).

Irrational behavior does not necessarily mean that the market is inefficient as long as the market acts rational (adjust quickly) as a whole. If some market participants are able to earn abnormal profit from irrational behavior of others, the market would be inefficient.

Biasness of loss aversion: It is the tendency of market participants to dislike losses more than they like equal gains. The under- reaction and overreaction anomalies may be explained with this behavioral biasness.

Herding: It is the tendency of investors to mimic the crowd or other investors in their investment decisions and ignore their own analysis and information. The under- reaction and overreaction anomalies may be explained with this behavioral biasness.

Overconfidence Bias: Sometimes investors tend to be overconfident in estimating the intrinsic value of a security which leads to mispricing.

Information cascade: The information moves from big and most informed investors to less and individual investors. The less informed investors act on that information. That is called information cascade. It is possible that the most informed investors can use less informed investors to move the prices.

Investors also suffer from other biasness like over optimism, over pessimism which results in market anomalies.

The behavioral finance tries to explain all these problems.

If you are enjoying this book s far kindly leave your honest reviews at
https://books2read.com/Equity-Investment-in-one-week-by-M-Imran-ahsan

Study session 13 Equity investment (2)

READING 39 OVERVIEW OF EQUITY SECUITY

LOS 39a: Describe characteristics of types of equity securities.

LOS 39b: Describe differences in voting rights and other ownership characteristics among different equity classes.

1. Preferred shared/stock: Preferred stock holders have higher seniority than common shares. When a company is liquidated or issues dividend, preferred stock holders are paid first. Preferred stock holders get dividends at specific rate usually as a percentage of par value. But typically they do not have any voting right.

Preferred stocks can be classified as equity or a financial liability depending on the circumstances. If preferred stock are perpetual and non-redeemable shares (cannot be bought back by company), then they are classified as equity. If they are redeemable on a fixed date at a certain price, they would be classed as a financial liability. When a company repurchases their own shares, they can hold or cancel them. When they hold shares those are called _treasury stocks_. Company can resell them in future if they hold them.

There are following reasons why a company buys its own stock

1. Management thinks shares are undervalued.
2. Shares are needed to meet employee stock option obligations.
3. Company wants to reduce or offset the dilution effect.

With **cumulative preferred** shares the company has to pay any missing dividend to preferred stock holders before paying anything to common stock holders. With **participating preferred** stock the preferred stock holders get additional dividends if company`s profits goes beyond a certain level. Preferred stocks can also be converted into common stocks at predetermined rate.

2. Common shares/stock: Common stock holders have residual claims on company's assets. It means they are paid at last (after paying liabilities, preferred stock holders etc).The Company issue common stock in return for the contributed capital. Number of authorized, issued and outstanding shares must be disclosed on the company's balance sheet under equity. **Authorized shares** are the number of shares which can be issued under company's article of incorporation. **Issued shares** are the number of shares issued to public. **Outstanding shares** are the issued shares minus number of shares company has purchased back (if any). The common stock holders have the ownership rights in the company. They have the voting rights to elect the board members, merger/acquisition decisions and related matters, so they involve in management of a company. The common stock holders can vote directly are can assign anybody to vote on their behalf. This is called <u>votes by proxy</u>. Under <u>statutory voting</u> system one common share has one vote. Under <u>cumulative voting</u> system the common stock holder can assign any number of votes to any electing board member. Companies can issue different classes of common shares with different voting and or ownership rights.

<u>Callable common</u> shares give the company the right to buy back its shares at a predetermined price (this option is exercised by companies when the market prices go up beyond strike price). <u>Put-able common</u> share give the right to shares holders to sell them at a predetermined price (this option is exercised by investors when the market prices go down beyond strike price).

Different classes of shares may have different voting powers and priority of dividends/payment at liquidation. The details about the voting and other rights can be available in company's filing with SECP.

LOS 39c: Distinguish between public and private equity securities.

When we discuss equity we usually mean public equity securities, issued by publically trading companies because the market for these securities is significantly larger than private securities.

Following are the differences between public and private equity securities.

Liquidity: The private equity securities are less liquid because there is no active market for them. This is usually compensated by higher return on investment.

Price: The prices of public equity securities are determined my market but the prices of private equities are negotiated and determined between parties.

Regulations: There is less disclosure requirements and other regulations involved in private equities than public equities.

Transparency: Private equity market is less transparent than public equity because of less disclosures and regulations.

Private equities are usually issued to sophisticated and institutional investors who fulfill some minimum criteria to protect unsophisticated investors. Also the private equity issuing companies face fewer costs as there are less disclosure requirements and fewer regulations to follow and costs related to issuing reports.

Investment in private companies (private equity securities) is made by following ways (but not limited to)

Leverage buyouts (LBOs): LBOs are the use of borrowed money to purchase shares of established companies.

Venture capital: In venture capital the investment is made in new companies who have great potential to grow (startups).

Distresses investment: In distressed investment the investors invest in companies who are financially distressed and desperately need funds.

Private investment in public company: This is the private purchase of shares of a public company that is in distress (secondary offering).Secondary offering is usually at considerable discount if the company is not working efficiently.

LOS 39d: Describe methods for investing in non-domestic equity securities.

With the inception of new technology the world has become global village. In this global village, the investors can invest in non-domestic securities with great ease at low cost. The companies can also raise capital from foreign investors now although some countries still restrict free capital flow to protect domestic stability and to reduce uncertainty. Following ways can be adopted to invest in non-domestic equities.

Direct investment: It means the investors can buy foreign securities in foreign markets. This also means that the investment and returns are in foreign currencies. The investor should be aware of the regulations and procedures of foreign market. The exchange rate can also play its roll (favorable or unfavorable). The foreign currency may or may not be liquid.

Depository receipts: A bank deposits the shares of a foreign firm and then issues depository receipts which represent ownership in foreign firm. These receipts trade like common share in local currency. The issuing bank is called custodian and manages the dividends, stock splits and other matters. The value of DR can be affected by exchange rate, foreign country's economic outlook and firm's own fundamentals. DR can be sponsored or unsponsored. With sponsored DR the holder of these receipts have the voting rights and is more regulated. With unsponsored DR the issuer bank retains the voting rights. There are two types of depository receipts: Global depository receipts and American depository receipts.

<u>Global depository receipts:</u> The DR issued outside of USA and the firm's own country, are called GDRs. The GDRs are not subject to the cash flow and foreign ownership restrictions imposed by the firm's domestic country. GDRs are mostly denominated in US Dollar. Due to fewer restrictions GDRs are of good attraction to foreign investors.

<u>American Depository Receipts:</u> A DR denominated in US dollar and trade like common share in US stock exchange is ADR. There are four major types of ADRs each required different trading level and other requirement.

Global Registered shares (GRS): These are the common shares being traded in different country's stock exchanges in domestic currencies.

Basket of listed depository receipts (BLDR): This is an exchange traded fund (ETF) which has portfolio of different depository receipts. BLDR trades like a common share. BLDR can be used to hedge and or arbitrage and it is very easy way to get foreign exposure.

LOS 39e: Compare the risk and return characteristics of different types of equity securities.

Different types of equities and their characteristics have different risk and returns associated with them.

Return of equity

Capital appreciation and dividends are two main sources of return on equity.

$$\text{Return on equity} = \frac{Ending\ price\ p1 - Begining\ price\ p0 + didvidends}{Begining\ price\ p0}$$

In case of direct investment in foreign equity markets, exchange rate movement (positive or negative) can also be a source. On the other hand reinvestment of dividends can also be a source of return.

Risk characteristics

Standard deviation is most common measure for risk calculation. Usually higher the risk is, higher the expected return. Preferred stock is less risky because they have priority of dividend payment over common stock. So the expected return of preferred stock is lower than common stock. Cumulative preferred stock is less risky than non-cumulative common stock because they also pay any missed dividend. Call-able common or preferred shares are riskier (for investor) than non-callable common or preferred shares because the issuer can call them. In same way put-able common or preferred shares are less risky than non-put-able common or preferred shares.

LOS 39f: Explain the role of equity securities in the financing of a company's assets.

When companies issue securities they raise capital and their liquidity increases. Companies issue equities for the following main reasons:

To purchase long term assets like property plant and equipments

- For research and development expenditures
- For expansion of business
- To launch new products
- To acquire other companies
- To give incentives to employees
- To meet capital requirements and related issues

LOS 39g: Distinguish between the market value and book value of equity securities.

Book value: Book value of equity securities reflects the historical decisions of management.

Book value = value of total assets – value of total liabilities

Book value increases with increase in, net income, retained earnings, total assets etc. Book value per common shares is the total book value divided by weighted average outstanding common shares.

Market value: Market value of equity is the value which is decided by investors collectively in the market. Investors decide the market value using fundamentals of a company, required rate of return (given its risk), all available information and future expectations about company. The book value and market value is rarely same. Although the management tries to maximize the book value of a company is does not necessarily reflect in the market value because the market value is mostly based on future return and risks associated with the company. If the market value to book value ratio of a company is higher than other companies in same industry it can be deduced that the investors expect high growth.

LOS 39h: Compare a company's cost of equity, its (accounting) return on equity, and investors' required rates of return.

Cost of equity and required rate of return: Cost of equity is the minimum rate of return a firm should offer to investors to purchase its shares in primary market. Usually cost of equity is calculated using CAPM and dividend discount models.

$$\text{Cost of equity using CAPM model} = E(Ri) = Rf + \beta i[E(Rm) - Rf]$$

$E(Ri)$ = expected rate of return on "i" security which is cost of equity to issuer.

Rf= Risk free rate of return

E(Rm) expected market rate of return

Bi= Beta of investment

Dividend discount model consider the current market price and expected future dividends of a security. The rate which equates all future dividends to its current market price is the cost of equity (also called **required rate of return**).

As RRR and share price are inversely related. An increase in RRR would reduce the share price and vice versa. It can also be explained in another way. A reduction in the price of equity will increase expected return.

Return on equity: Return on equity is used to determine the management's efficiency in using capital to generate profits.

$$ROE = \frac{Net\ income\ at\ end\ of\ year}{Book\ value\ at\ the\ beging\ of\ the\ year} = \frac{NI}{BV0}$$

We can use average of book values (BV at beginning and book value at end of the year) if it is volatile.

If you are enjoying this book s far kindly leave your honest reviews at
https://books2read.com/Equity-Investment-in-one-week-by-M-Imran-ahsan

READING 40: INTRODUCTION TO INDUSTRY AND COMPANY ANALYSIS

LOS 40a: Explain uses of industry analysis and the relation of industry analysis to company analysis.

Industry analysis helps an analyst to understand what's happening in the industry. Industry analysis is very important in understanding of a company's business environment. It plays a pivotal role in stock valuation and credit analysis. It also helps the analyst to decide which company in a specific industry to focus on (usually more useful for active investors). Sometimes a company may have huge potential to perform but the industry of that company is in downfall. In this situation the shares of that company may not give us expected results. This can be avoided and forecasted through industry analysis.

LOS 40b: Compare methods by which companies can be grouped, current industry classification systems, and classify a company, given a description of its activities and the classification system.

Usually companies are classified with respect to the product or services they are producing by using principle of their main business activities or the largest source of revenues for a business. The companies are also classified with respect to the sensitivity of business cycle and statistical similarities. According to "Sensitivity of business cycle" classification the companies are classified as cyclical and non-cyclical companies. A cyclical company is one whose revenues are strongly dependent on macroeconomic conditions of an economy. Non-cyclical or defensive companies are those which are independent of business cycle. The firms are also classified according to statistical similarities. In this classification the firms whose returns are highly correlated (historically) with each other are grouped together (cluster analysis). There would be less correlation between groups.

Current industry classification systems and commercial industry classification systems

Global industry classification standard is created by S&P and MSCI Barra. In this classification companies are classified according to their main business activity and into subcategories. Russel Global Sectors classification classifies the companies on the basis of products or services. Industry Classification Benchmark is created by Dow Jones and FTSE. In this index companies are categorized based on their primary source of revenue. Commercial classification can be described as follows.

Basic materials and processing: **This category includes following sub-categories**

- Building materials
- Chemicals
- Paper
- Forest products
- Containers and packaging
- Metal
- Mineral
- Mining companies

Consumer discretionary: These are considered as cyclical consumer-related products or services. They include

- Automotive
- Hotel and restaurants
- Apparels

Consumer staples: These are considered as non-cyclical industries and include

- Food,
- Drugs,
- Beverages,
- Tobacco,
- basic household products

Energy: These firms include exploration, production, refining and other services related to energy products.

Financial services: In this classification the firms are involved in

- Banking
- Insurance
- Finance
- Real estate
- Asset management
- Brokerage

Healthcare

These firms are involved in medical products and services like

- Pharmaceuticals
- Biotech
- Medical supplies and equipments

Industrial and producer durables:

These firms provide capital goods and commercial services like

- Heavy machinery
- Defense
- Transportation

Technology: These firms are involved in

- Software development
- Computers and computer related equipments and devices
- Internet equipments
- Semiconductors

Telecommunications: These firms provide telecommunication services with wire or wireless.

Utilities: These firms provide utilities like gas, electricity etc.

Government industry classifications

Government bodies also classify companies for data analysis and to compare different industries.

International Standard Industrial Classification of All Economic Activities (ISIC): is used by United Nations in 1948 to compare different industries globally. It is classifies firms according to their main business activity.

Statistical Classification of Economic Activities in the European Community: It is like ISIC but used for European firms only.

Australian and New Zealand Standard Industrial Classification: It is used by Australia and New Zealand.

North American Industry Classification System (NAICS): It is developed by USA, Canada and Mexico.

Difference between commercial and government industry classifications

Commercial classification system is more frequently updated while government bodies update less frequently.

Commercial classification systems identify individual companies. Analysts can indentify constituent firms in commercial system while government systems do not identify individual firms in a group.

Another difference is the government systems group all the firms in an industry including non-profit organizations while commercial system only include companies whose main motive is profit.

LOS 40c: Explain the factors that affect the sensitivity of a company to the business cycle and the uses and limitations of industry and company descriptors such as "growth," "defensive," and "cyclical".

Cyclical firm faces higher (than average) demand in expansion phase while lower (than average) demand during contraction phase of business cycle so does their profits. Cyclical firms can include Auto industry, Housing, technology etc.

Non-cyclical firms face relatively stable demand during any phase of business cycle. Non-cyclical firms provide utilities, food, healthcare etc.

Grouping companies with respect to sensitivity to business cycle can give an analyst the insight of a firm's performance in different economic phases. In a period of 'boom' a higher than average performance of a cyclical firm cannot be given much importance.

Non-cyclical firms can be further classified as "defensive" and "growth". Defensive firms are least affected by business cycle while growth firms are those which are not affected by business cycle as their demand is too high. They have high growth potential and do not usually pay dividends (as they reinvest their earnings).

The terms 'cyclical', defensive and growth must be used with caution. A firm can be cyclical with growth potential. Another firm can be defensive with growth. A non-cyclical firm may be affected in severe recession. A multinational firm can be growing on one market and while in downfall in another country or market. Another problem with grouping is' the phenomena of business cycle sensitivity is continuous (not constant).

LOS 40d: Explain how a company's industry classification can be used to identify a potential "peer group" for equity valuation.

Peer group: A peer group is a set of companies that share similar characteristics like cost structure, demand, business activities, size etc. Peer group is used for comparison and evaluation.

To form a peer group an analyst should identify companies from same group classification (commercial classification).

Other information should also be used to verify whether the companies really belong to peer group or not. In forming a peer group analyst should go through annual reports of a company and its competitors, and industry publications.

Steps to form peer group

- Use commercial classification system.
- Go thorough firm's and its competitors' annual reports in same industry.
- Check that all the companies you intend to include in peer group have same source of revenues, similar cost structures and they also identify each other as competitors.
- Make adjustments for a company with 'finance' subsidiaries if they have any.

LOS 40e: Describe the elements that need to be covered in a thorough industry analysis.

Following elements should be included in thorough industry analysis;

- Analyze the forces that may affect the industry's profitability and performance like macroeconomic variables, geographical circumstances, political and governmental forces, social and technological changes.

- Competitive scenario: Threat of new entry and substitution, bargaining power of customer should be analyzed.

- Use the historical evaluation of the industry to analyze the performance of industry especially different phases of business cycle.

- Classify the firms in 'strategic groups'. A strategic group consists of different companies that share distinctively same characteristics and are in same life-cycle phase (embryonic, growth, mature etc.).

- Place the industry on *experience curve*. An experience curve shows cost per unit with respect to output.

- Evaluate and estimate the industry variables using different models.

LOS 40f: Describe the principles of strategic analysis of an industry.

Some industries earn economic profit while others do not. The economic profit is the excess return on invested capital minus cost of capital. The economic profit highly depends on firm's market competition and its pricing power. Strategic analysis is a tool to measure "competitive environment of an industry and how industry's competitive environment influences a firm's strategy. " A framework developed by Peter called "Peter's fives forces" can be used to determine competitive environment.

According to Peter there are following five determinants of competition in an industry:

Threat of entry: If there is less threat of new entry, the existing firms would hold significant pricing power and can earn economic profits. The barriers of new entry can be huge initial cost, economics and scale or the governmental restricts. The analyst should carefully examine these factors.

Rivalry among existing firms: The existing firms also compete with each other for market share. When there are more firms of same size in an industry the competition would be tough and there will be less pricing power.

Bargaining power of supplier: If the raw material suppliers have more bargaining power they will raise the prices, lower the quality and reduce the quantity. Bargaining power of supplier increases if there are limited numbers of suppliers exist in the market.

Bargaining power of buyers: The buyers can also exert pressure on the businesses to reduce prices, increase quality and better after sale services. All these elements reduce profitability. Sometimes governments also pressurize the firms to reduce the prices and increase quality of healthcare and transportation types of businesses.

Threat of substitutes: Availability of substitutes increases the price elasticity and the firms cannot charge high prices. Moreover the firms can feel if they will charge high price there would be more firms entering in the market and will take away their share. This factor also limits their pricing power.

LOS 40g: Explain the effects of barriers to entry, industry concentration, industry capacity, and market share stability on pricing power and price competition.

Barriers to entry: When the barriers to entry are higher it may means the existing firms have pricing power. New entrants take away the market share and the profits of existing firms. If the same firms remains in a market for longer time we can assume high barriers to entry. More the products are differentiated in the market, more to existing firms have pricing power. If there is tough competition among existing firms then high barriers to entry cannot guarantee high pricing power. This usually happens when the products are not differentiated. Moreover there may be high capital cost to enter and or exit in from the market and the existing firms could be in losses (or not making economic profits) but they are operating in a hope that one day the situation will change. Some business like utilities may have high barriers to enter but they could be under high influence of government to not charge high prices.

Barriers to entry can also change over time. In another situation, sometimes the buyers have significant bargaining power so the barriers to entry cannot be the single factor for the pricing power. However it observed that the higher the barriers to entry more the firms have pricing power.

Industry concentration: Higher industry concentration means some firms have higher market share. Usually higher concentration means more pricing power but a number of other factors should be analyzed before concluding that.

- If one firms has 50% market share (which is very high) but if there is only one other firm which also has other 50% of market share, the 50% share of one firm does not give any pricing power to any firm. So the market share must be analyzed in relative to the competitors. A firm with 15% market share may have high pricing power because the competitors have only 2 or 3 % market share.
- In a market where one firm has more market share but all the firms are producing undifferentiated products, the pricing power is too low as the customers can move to other firms without any hesitation.
- When the exit from the market is very costly, high concentration does not give any pricing power.
- When the existing firms coordinate with each other they can charge higher prices.

Industry capacity: When the firms are in under capacity situation (demand is higher than supply) they have more pricing power. In a situation of overcapacity (supply is higher than demand) the firms have no pricing power. When the firms are under capacity an analyst should examine how much time firms can take to satisfy unsatisfied demand. In a capital intensive industry it takes years to build new plants and machinery to produce more. It should also be considered how the existing firms are planning to fulfill excessive demand.

Market share stability: It should be carefully examined whether the market share of the firms is stable over time or not. If the share is stable it means the industry is less competitive and the firms have more pricing power. When the market share fluctuates over time it means that the industry is competitive. More competitive the industry is, lesser the pricing power firms have. Market share stability can be a function of innovation, barriers to entry and switching cost. Switching cost means the time and efforts customers exert in order to know about products of competitors. Higher the switching cost is more stable the market share of the firms.

LOS 40h: Describe industry life cycle models, classify an industry as to life cycle stage, and describe limitations of the life-cycle concept in forecasting industry performance.

Industry's life cycle is important part of strategic analysis because stage of an industry has impact on its competitiveness, growth and ultimately on profits. As the stage changes, the above three (competitiveness, growth and profits) also changes so the industry should be analyzed as ongoing basis. There are five stages of an industry;

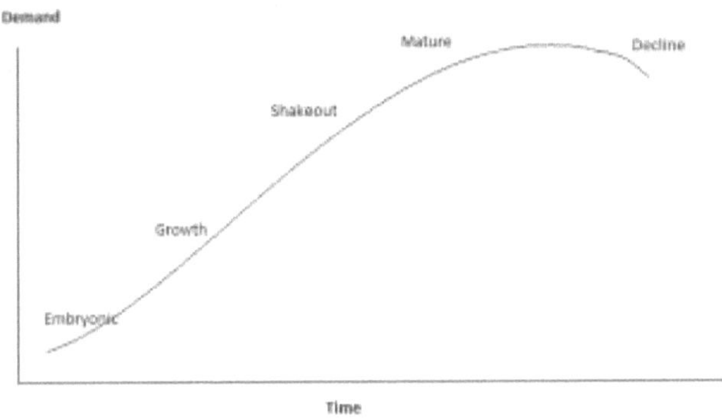

1. **Embryonic:** This is the stage when an industry has just started.

This stage has following characteristics;

- Slow growth
- High prices
- Low volumes and sales
- High failure risk
- Need of huge investment

1. **Growth stage:** In this stage the customers start discovering the product. There is less competition but the threat of new entry in imminent. Following are the characteristics of this stage:

- Falling prices,
- Rapid increase in demand,
- Increase in profitability
- Minimum competition

1. **Shakeout stage:** In this stage the growth is slow because of tough competition and there are fewer customers to be added. So the profitability falls. At this stage the industry focus on cost reduction.

1. **Mature:**

- Little or no growth
- Consolidation of firms into oligopoly (superior firms will get more market share)
- High barriers of entry
- Stable profits and pricing

1. **Decline stage:**

- Negative growth

- Falling pricing due to over capacity and intense competition
- Firms began to merge or exit from the market

Limitations

Careful analysis is required in classification of industry in its stages and the performances of individual firms. Sometimes a firm may not behave according to the stage of the industry. A firm may be in profit while the overall industry is falling apart. The firm may be in different stage than the overall industry. There are other factors which can affect a firm like innovation, regulatory and legal issues, geographical factors etc.

LOS 40i: Compare characteristics of representative industries from the various economic sectors.

The following elements should be included in a comparison:

- Major companies
- Barriers to entry
- Concentration within an industry
- Impact of industry capacity on pricing
- Industry stability; How often and quickly the market share changes
- Life cycle; Embryonic or mature etc
- Price and other competition
- Demographic influences
- Regulatory or governmental influences; quality and quantity of regulations
- Social influences
- Technological influences
- Sensitivity to business cycle

LOS 40j: Describe macroeconomic, technological, demographic, governmental, and social influences on industry growth, profitability, and risk.

The macroeconomic, technological, demographic, governmental, and social factors can influence the industry growth, profitability and risks. All these factors should be included in strategic analysis.

Macroeconomic factors: A structural change or phases of a business cycle in an economy directly affect the industry's growth, profitability and risks. Industries are affected by interest rates, inflation, availability of credit and overall GDP. A structural change, like introduction of new and better ways of production, can hit and industry in a good way.

Technological Influences: A change in technology can introduce new and better products and the related industries can be influenced dramatically. For example, development of smart phones has changed many industries like photography, cassette players and desktop computers.

Demographic influences: Composition of population like, age distribution, gender distribution and population size can affect the industries. Increase in population can increase the demand of almost all industries. Increase in the young population can increase the demand for new trendy clothing and shoes etc.

Governmental influences: Governments can significantly affect industries through taxation and other regulatory controls. Some industries like tobacco and alcohol can be heavily taxed while heath care and food industry can be highly regularized.

Social influences: Social norms and the behavior of people affect different industries. For example, when more people tend eat out, the food industry grows.

LOS 40k: Describe the elements that should be covered in a thorough company analysis.

A thorough company analysis must include, analysis of company's financial statements, products/services being provided by the firm and its competitive strategy. Competitive strategy is how the firm responds to the external threats and opportunities.

There are two main competitive strategies; low cost strategy or cost leadership and product differentiation. According to Porter, a firm must adopt one strategy from these two in order to be successful.

A thorough company analysis should include following items;

- Firm's overview: information about firm's, operations, products/services, current position sales composition, product life-cycle etc.

- Relevant industry characteristics: Life cycle stages, business cycle sensitivity, entry and exit barriers, industry concentration, product differentiation, brand loyalty, customer and buyer relations, opportunities, technology in use etc.

- Demand

- Supply

- Pricing power

- Financial rations like return on equity

If you are enjoying this book s far kindly leave your honest reviews at https://books2read.com/Equity-Investment-in-one-week-by-M-Imran-ahsan

READING 41: EQUITY VALUATION: CONCEPTS AND BASIC TOOLS

LOS 41a: Evaluate whether a security, given its current market price and a value estimate, is overvalued, fairly valued, or undervalued by the market.

When

Current market value > estimated value; the security is overvalued

Current market value < estimated value; the security is undervalued

Current market value = estimated value; the security is fairly valued

Analysts should take great care and use different models to estimate the value of a security (its intrinsic value). A good analyst looks at the market price with skepticism but with respect. Because the market value is decided by all investors collectively and a price deviation from intrinsic value may be result of an error in calculation.

LOS 41b: Describe major categories of equity valuation models.

Analysts usually use many models to estimate the intrinsic value of a security.

There are three categories of equity valuation models;

- Discounted cash flow/ Dividend discount models/present value models
- Multiplier models/market multiplier models
- Asset-based valuation models

Discounted cash flow/ Dividend discount models/present value models: In this model all the future expected cash flows are discounted to get the present value of a security. These cash flows can include dividends, free cash flow to equity etc.

Multiplier models/market multiplier models: There are two basic types of multiplier models 1. Ration of market price to some fundamentals like earnings (P/E) or to book value (P/BV) etc. The results can be examined in absolute terms are compared with industry peer group. For example a higher P/E ratio could indicate high growth prospects in future. Second multiplier model uses the ratio of enterprise value to EBITDA or revenues (i.e. enterprise value /EBITDA).

Enterprise Value = Market cap + Total debt – Cash & cash equivalents

Asset-based valuation models: In this model the book value is used to estimate intrinsic value of a security.

Book value = Total assets – total liabilities

When we get the book value we can divide it by number of outstanding shares to get per share book value.

LOS 41c: Describe regular cash dividends, extra dividends, stock dividends, stock splits, reverse stock splits, and share repurchases.

Dividends: Any distribution to the shareholders.

Following are some aspects of dividends

Cash dividends: Payment to the shareholders in cash. Sometimes companies pay _regular dividends_ on quarterly, semiannually or annual basis. A regular dividend shows that the company is sound.

Extra dividends: When a company earns higher profits in a favorable situation the management can decide to pay extra dividends (in spite of regular dividends) to supplement to regular dividends.

Stock dividends: Dividends paid in stock (rather than cash) is called stock dividend. For example a company announces 20% stock dividend, every common stock holder will get extra 20 shares per 100 shares. In case of stock dividend, total outstanding shares increases, value of each share may be less now while the cost of shares (for shareholder) decreases as the shareholders get the new shares free of cost. The proportionate ownership of shareholders in the company remains same.

Stock splits: In stock split the company splits existing outstanding shares in multiple shares. For example a stock split 4 for one means every shareholder who has 1 common stock will get 4 shares. The price and value of shares decrease proportionately. For example 2 for one split will decrease the value and price of a stock to 50%. Overall the market cap and the ownership of shareholders do not change. Stock splits are usually done to increase liquidity in secondary market.

Reverse stock splits: This is opposite to stock split. In reverse stock split the company reduces number of outstanding shares. For example a reverse stock split of 1 for 2 means a common stock holder who has 2 shares will have one share. Total wealth of shareholders remains same as the value and price increase proportionately.

Share repurchase: In share repurchase a company buys back its shares for common stock holders. These purchased shares cannot be used in voting or dividend payments. As these are not outstanding shares any more they are not used in earning per share calculation. This usually happens when the shares are undervalued in the market. This is considered just like a cash dividends of equal value. Companies also do this to reduce the number of outstanding shares or when the capital gain is taxed at lower rate than dividends.

LOS 41d: Describe dividend payment chronology.

The dates related to the dividend payment are collectively called dividend payment chronology. The order is as following

Declaration date

Ex-dividend date

Holder of Record date

Payment date

Declaration date: The date at which company declares its intentions to pay dividend. The dividends are declared on the approval of directors. On declaration date holder of record date, amount of dividend and the payment dates are also announced.

Ex-dividend date (or ex-date): The date on or after which the buyer of stock will not get the next dividend. It means if an investor buys a stock on or after the ex-dividend date he/she will not get next dividend. The ex-date is usually one or two business days before the *holder of record date.*

Holder of Record date: It is the date on which the holders of a stock are considered as the stockholders and will get the dividend.

Payment date: It is the date at which the dividends are mailed or transferred to the stockholders. It may or may not be a business day.

LOS 41e: Explain the rationale for using present value models to value equity and describe the dividend discount and free-cash-flow-to-equity models.

The present value model shows that the value of an investment today should be the present value of all future benefits.

Dividend discount model proposes that the value of an investment today (intrinsic value) is the present value of expected future dividends and final payment (if any).

$$V0 = \sum_{t=1}^{n} \frac{Dt}{(1+r)^t} + \frac{Pn}{(1+r)^n}$$

V0= value of an investment today (present value)

Dt= Expected dividend in period t

r= Discounting factor or required rate of return

P= Terminal price at the liquidation time of security

In case of common stock there is no terminal value but we can use an expected terminal value in future when we expect to sale our stock (considering growth rate of the security)

As the investors are sacrificing present consumption for future benefits the present value must be the discounted cash flows of future benefits.

Free cash-flows-to-equity models: This model is based on the future capacity of a company to pay dividends. Free cash-flows-to-equity (FCFE) is the cash available for common stock holders after paying all obligations and fixed capital expenditures.

FCFE = Net income + Non-cash expenses – increase in working capital –Fixed capital investment + net borrowing

Or

FCFE = Cash flow from operations – Fixed capital investment + net borrowing

Net borrowing means debt borrowed minus debt paid.

We can use same discounting formula using FCFE;

$$V0 = \sum_{t=1}^{n} \frac{(FCFE)t}{(1+r)^t}$$

LOS 41f: Calculate the intrinsic value of a non-callable, non-convertible preferred stock.

The intrinsic value of a non-callable, non-convertible preferred stock can be calculated as we calculate intrinsic value of a common stock (here we will terminal value in form of par value)

$$V0 = \sum_{t=1}^{n} \frac{Dt}{(1+r)^t} + \frac{(PAR)n}{(1+r)^n}$$

Where
    PAR is the par value.
    'n' is the years of maturity.
    V0= present value
    Dt= Expected dividend in period t
    r= Discounting factor or required rate of return

LOS 41g: Calculate and interpret the intrinsic value of an equity security based on the Gordon (constant) growth dividend discount model or a two-stage dividend discount model, as appropriate.

Gordon (constant) growth dividend discount model: This model assumes that the dividends grow at a constant rate. It implies that the next year dividend (D1) is

    $D1 = D0(1+ g)$

Where g is growth rate of dividend and D0 is current dividend and D1 is dividend at period 1.

    And

$$D2 = D1(1+g) \quad \text{or } D2 = D0(1+g)^2 \quad \text{and so one}$$

So the intrinsic value V0 (the present value) is

$$V0 = \frac{D0(1+g)}{(1+r)} + \frac{D0((1+g)^2}{(1+r)^2} \frac{D0((1+g)^3}{(1+r)^3} \cdots \cdots \frac{D0((1+g)^n}{(1+r)^n}$$

Or
$$V0 = \frac{D0(1+g)}{(r-g)} = \frac{D1}{(r-g)}$$

The growth rate g= b x return on equity

'b'= earnings retention rate or (1- dividend payout rate) x ROE

<u>Assumptions of constant growth model:</u>

- The dividend grows at a constant rate.
- Required rate of return is constant throughout a company's life.
- 'r' is always greater than 'g' otherwise the equation will not work
- Dividends are a good measure for the company's health and wealth.

Multistage dividend discount model: When a company's current dividend growth rate is higher and it seemed unsustainable, two stage or multistage DDM is used. This model has two parts one is for short period of unstable dividends and other is for long term dividend payments when the company is stable and it pays dividends which grow at a constant rate.

We can sum up the two stage formula as follows:

$$V0 = \sum_{t=1}^{n} \frac{D0(1+gs)^t}{(1+r)^t} + \frac{D0(1+gs)^n(1-gl)}{(1+r)^n(r-gl)}$$

'n' is the number of years of short term unstable growth

'gs' is the short term growth rate

'gl' is long term growth rate

'r' is the required rate of return

LOS 41h: Identify characteristics of companies for which the constant growth or a multistage dividend discount model is appropriate.

Constant growth model is useful to evaluate a company which is stable, paying divided with a stable growth and is insensitive to business cycle

The two stage or multistage growth model is used when the company is paying dividends but they are deemed highly unstable, rapidly growing currently for some time and are sensitive to business cycle.

LOS 41i: Explain the rationale for using price multiples to value equity, how the price to earnings multiple relates to fundamentals, and the use of multiples based on comparables.

The DDM and present value models are highly sensitive to required rate of return and other inputs, the analysts also use price multipliers in estimating the intrinsic value. The famous price multipliers are price to book value (P/BV) price to earnings (P/E) price to sales (P/Sales) price to cash flow etc and these multipliers are used to compare with industry average and peers group. If the fundaments of two companies are same they should have same price multipliers (law of one price). Some criticize on use of historical price and sales date so the projected data can be used for example next year's expected earnings (based on historical growth and other factors).

LOS 41j: Calculate and interpret the following multiples: price to earnings, price to an estimate of operating cash flow, price to sales, and price to book value.

Price to earnings (P/E): Mostly used price multiplier. It is calculated as market price divided by earnings per share. It tells us about the undervalued or overvalued company relatively to the industry.

Generally a lower P/E ratio will generate higher return in future, but it can also be a symbol of lower expected growth.

Price to an estimate of operating cash flow (P/CF): It is calculated ad market price of a share divided by operating cash flow per share (or free cash flow per share). It is useful for the companies having positive cash flows. It tells us how much cash flows are generated by the company relative to its price. Some says this metric is better than P/E because the earnings can be easily manipulated than cash flows. Some companies can show earnings but may not be generating enough cash flows.

Price to sales (P/S): Market price of share divided by sales per share. It tells us how much a company is earning relative to its stock price.

Price to book value (P/BV): It is calculated as market price divided by book value per share. It tells us what is the value of assets (after paying all obligations) of a company relative to its price.

LOS 41k: Describe enterprise value multiples and their use in estimating equity value.

Enterprise value usually means "what is the cost of to acquire a company".

EV= (market price per common stock x number of outstanding shares) + (market price of per preferred share x number of outstanding preferred shares) + Market value of debt – cash and cash equivalents – short term investments

EV/EBITDA: The most common EV multiple in use. An EV/EBITDA lower than 10 is viewed as healthy. This multiple is also useful when the net income is negative. But use of EBITDA (instead of net income) has a disadvantage; it includes non-cash items like depreciation etc.

EV/Operating income: When the market value of debt is hard to find, operating income can be a good alternative of EBITDA.

LOS 41l: Describe asset-based valuation models and their use in estimating equity value.

Asset based valuation is useful with the firms having less or insignificant intangible assets. In theory the value of the firm should be equal to the value of its assets minus its liabilities. Analysts usually use assets based valuation in combination with other valuation models. The intangible assets are hard to measure and can be under or overestimated.

The assets on balance sheet may also not depict the exact value especially in inflationary environment. Analysts usually use inflation adjusted value of assets or replacement costs in evaluation. Some other factors like customer satisfaction, relationships with the buyers cannot be easily and reliably estimated (but they have significant power to influence the profitability).

LOS 41.m: Explain advantages and disadvantages of each category of valuation model.

Free cash flow to equity model

Advantages:

- A very good and close estimate of intrinsic value of a stock
- It can be a trustworthy estimate than relative valuation models
- Well defined and being used in finance

Disadvantages:
If projected cash flow estimates are wrong a bad stock may look good

Very sensitive to inputs especially to required rate of return

Gordon constant growth dividend model

Advantages:

- Simple calculation
- Easy to compare different companies of different sizes
- Widely used in finance

Disadvantages:

- Does not cover important factors like brand loyalty and relationships with suppliers etc.
- It assumes that the dividends will grow at a constant rate which is not usually the case

Multistage dividend discount mode:

Advantages:

- Better estimates than constant growth model
- More flexible in measuring the value of a company

Disadvantages:

- Complex calculations
- Depends much on estimates

Multiplier models

Advantages:

- Calculations are easy
- Give us useful information about the company
- Can be used to compare different companies
- Fairly good predictors of company's future

Disadvantages:

- A price lag can give us wrong predictions
- Mispricing can also be an issue

Asset-based valuation model

Advantages:

- Simple calculation
- Usually no projection is required
- Can be used with other models
- Useful in evaluation of companies with more tangible and less intangible assets

Disadvantages:

- Cannot be used in isolation without using other evaluation models, otherwise the estimation can guide us wrongly

- It cannot be much reliable because the market value of different assets may be different than on balance sheet.

That's all for the Equity investments Level 1 2020. Please leave review about this book at

https://books2read.com/Equity-Investment-in-one-week-by-M-Imran-ahsan

Don't miss out!

Visit the website below and you can sign up to receive emails whenever M. Imran Ahsan publishes a new book. There's no charge and no obligation.

https://books2read.com/r/B-A-ZWUK-EKAGB

BOOKS2READ

Connecting independent readers to independent writers.

Did you love *Equity Investment for CFA level 1*? Then you should read *Corporate Finance for CFA level 1*[1] by M. Imran Ahsan!

[2]

Make smart decisions and learn complete Corporate Finance for CFA level 1 in just one week. This book is written in simple and plain language to ensure that the students can grasp the concepts with great ease.

As a University instructor for the past 10 years, I know how to make things easy and understandable.

I am happy to launch this book with which you can cover and master the Corporate Finance part of CFA Level 1 with great ease. Nevertheless, this is most affordable and high-quality study material.

I look forward to come up with more books. Love you all the aspirants, and may you succeed in your goals.

---

1. https://books2read.com/u/bW1w97

2. https://books2read.com/u/bW1w97

Also by M. Imran Ahsan

ACCA
AACA: Business & Technology

CFA level 1
Corporate Finance for CFA level 1
Equity Investment for CFA level 1
CFA level 1 Fixed Income
Economics for CFA level 1 in just one week

Investment series
Corporate Finance: A Beginner's Guide
Fixed Income Securities: A Beginner's Guide to Understand, Invest and
Evaluate Fixed Income Securities

About the Author

I am a PhD scholar and is a university lecturer for more than 11 years. I have been teaching Finance and Economics at various levels.

As an instructor I believe in simplicity, comprehensivity and in conciseness. I believe in smart kind of hard work. It means you should use your time efficiently to achieve optimal goals with limited time and efforts.